CONTENTS

SPRINGING INTO ACTION

A rattlesnake rests in the sun on top of a dusty desert rock. The **predator** keeps quiet as a mouse scurries closer. Suddenly the snake **strikes** its **prey**. The mouse had no time to see the snake before it attacked.

Snakes eat many types of prey such as mice, birds and pigs. A snake's diet depends on its size. Big snakes can eat large prey. Smaller snakes eat smaller prey.

FACT

Brazil's Snake Island has so many deadly snakes that humans are not allowed to live there.

predator animal that hunts other animals for food

strike attack quickly

prey animal hunted by another animal for food

HUNT –

by Tammy Gagne

raintree
a Capstone company — publishers for children

527 625 49 6

Raintree is an imprint of Capstone Global Library Limited, a company incorporated in England and Wales having its registered office at 264 Banbury Road, Oxford, OX2 7DY – Registered company number: 6695582

www.raintree.co.uk
myorders@raintree.co.uk

Editorial Credits
Brenda Haugen, editor; Juliette Peters, designer; Tracy Cummins, media researcher; Katy LaVigne, production specialist

Printed and bound in China.

ISBN 978 1 474 70198 3 (hardback)
19 18 17 16 15
10 9 8 7 6 5 4 3 2 1

ISBN 978 1 474 70205 8 (paperback)
20 19 18 17 16
10 9 8 7 6 5 4 3 2 1

British Library Cataloguing in Publication Data
A full catalogue record for this book is available from the British Library.

Photo Credits
Alamy: blickwinkel, 6; Dreamstime: Maria Dryfhout, 9; Getty Images: John Cancalosi, 19, Roger de la Harpe, 3; iStockphoto: tirc83, 15; Science Source: Anthony Bannister, 21, Yoshiharu Sekino, 7; Shutterstock: chamleunejai, 17, pashabo, Design Element, reptiles4all, 11, Ryan M. Bolton, 1, Skynavin, Cover, Steve Byland, 2, 5, Cover Back, Trahcus, 18; SuperStock: Animals Animals, 12, NHPA, 16, Scubazoo, 14; Thinkstock: Mark Kostich, 13.

Every effort has been made to contact copyright holders of material reproduced in this book. Any omissions will be rectified in subsequent printings if notice is given to the publisher.

All the internet addresses (URLs) given in this book were valid at the time of going to press. However, due to the dynamic nature of the internet, some addresses may have changed, or sites may have changed or ceased to exist since publication. While the author and publisher regret any inconvenience this may cause readers, no responsibility for any such changes can be accepted by either the author or the publisher.

THE BIG SQUEEZE

Constrictors use their size and strength to overpower prey. These snakes wrap their bodies around their prey. Then they squeeze the prey until it stops breathing.

The largest constrictor is the giant anaconda. This powerful predator can be more than 6 metres (20 feet) long and weighs 136 kilograms (300 pounds). It is strong enough to kill a jaguar.

yellow anaconda

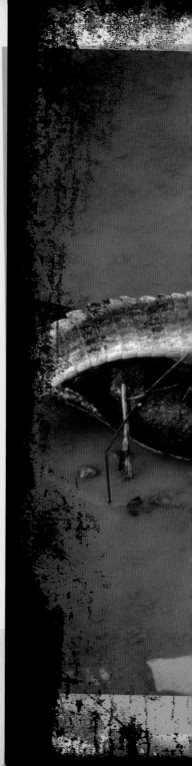

constrictor type of snake that wraps its body around prey and squeezes

An anaconda squeezes its prey in Venezuela.

DEADLY VENOM

Not all powerful predators are large. Some **venomous** snakes are less than 61 centimetres (2 feet) long. But don't be fooled by their small size. These snakes kill their prey by **injecting** venom through their **fangs**. Rattlesnakes, vipers and cobras are venomous snakes.

FACT

The inland taipan is the most venomous snake in the world. One bite from this snake produces enough venom to kill 250,000 mice!

venomous able to produce a harmful substance called venom

inject put into

fang long, hollow tooth; venom flows through fangs

venom

TASTING AND TRACKING

Snakes use their sense of taste to find prey. A snake has a special body part in the roof of its mouth called a Jacobson's organ. It works with the animal's tongue to taste **particles** in the air. By flicking its tongue out, a snake can find and track its prey.

FACT

Pit vipers are venomous snakes that have holes in their faces. The holes help the snakes to sense heat from nearby animals at night.

particle tiny piece of something

ON THE ATTACK

Snakes are known as **ambush** predators. They don't waste energy chasing prey. Snakes stay still until prey is within striking distance. Then they strike in a quick motion. The striking distance of most snakes is about half the length of their bodies.

death adder

FACT

The death adder **lures** its prey closer. The snake wiggles the worm-like tip of its tail to attract lizards and birds.

ambush surprise attack

lure attract something

CATCH ME IF YOU CAN!

Snakes can move quickly. The black mamba can travel across land at 20 kilometres (12.5 miles) per hour. It can also strike quickly. Its amazing speed helps the snake to catch prey. But like other snakes, black mambas wait for food to come close before attacking.

FACT

Sea snakes have flat tails that help them to swim quickly to catch fish.

banded sea snake

black mamba

OPEN WIDE

Most snakes can eat animals several times wider than their own heads. A snake's jaws open very wide. This ability lets a snake swallow its prey whole. The green anaconda is the largest snake in the world. It eats wild pigs, deer and jaguars.

FACT

The easiest meal for a snake to eat is a smaller snake. This is because the animals are the same shape. But not all types of snake eat other snakes.

green anaconda

anaconda

BE PATIENT!

Larger animals sometimes live for a short time after a venomous snake bites them. Venom from some snakes **paralyzes** prey. The prey isn't able to breathe and dies quickly. Most snakes wait for prey to die before eating it. Snakes can be hurt by eating prey that is still alive.

paralyze make someone or something unable to move

CLIMBING TREES

Snakes hunt in many ways. Some snakes even climb trees. They squeeze their muscles to hold onto tree trunks. The black rat snake hides inside empty woodpecker holes. When a bird or other prey animal comes near, the snake quickly claims its victim.

AMAZING BUT TRUE!

Venom from the boomslang snake stops blood from **clotting**. A bite from this African snake can cause its prey to bleed to death. The prey dies quickly from the venomous bite, but the snake does not wait for it to happen. The boomslang begins eating straight away.

clot become thicker and more solid; blood clots to stop the body from bleeding

GLOSSARY

ambush surprise attack

clot become thicker and more solid; blood clots to stop the body from bleeding

constrictor type of snake that wraps its body around prey and squeezes

fang long, hollow tooth; venom flows through fangs

inject put into

lure attract something

paralyze make someone or something unable to move

particle tiny piece of something

predator animal that hunts other animals for food

prey animal hunted by another animal for food

strike attack quickly

venomous able to produce a harmful substance called venom

READ MORE

Anaconda (A Day in the Life: Rainforest Animals),
Anita Ganeri (Raintree, 2011)

Amazing Animal Senses (Animal Superpowers),
John Townsend (Raintree, 2013)

Reptiles (Animal Classification), Angela Royston
(Raintree, 2015)

WEBSITES

www.bbc.co.uk/nature/life/Elapidae

Find out more about cobras, black mambas, inland taipans and more!

www.chesterzoo.org/animals/reptiles

Find out more about reptiles.

www.paigntonzoo.org.uk/animals-plants/animals/details/green-green-anaconda

Learn about the green anaconda.

COMPREHENSION QUESTIONS

1. What do snakes eat? Does a snake's body limit the size of prey it can eat?

2. What is a constrictor? How do constrictors hunt prey?

INDEX